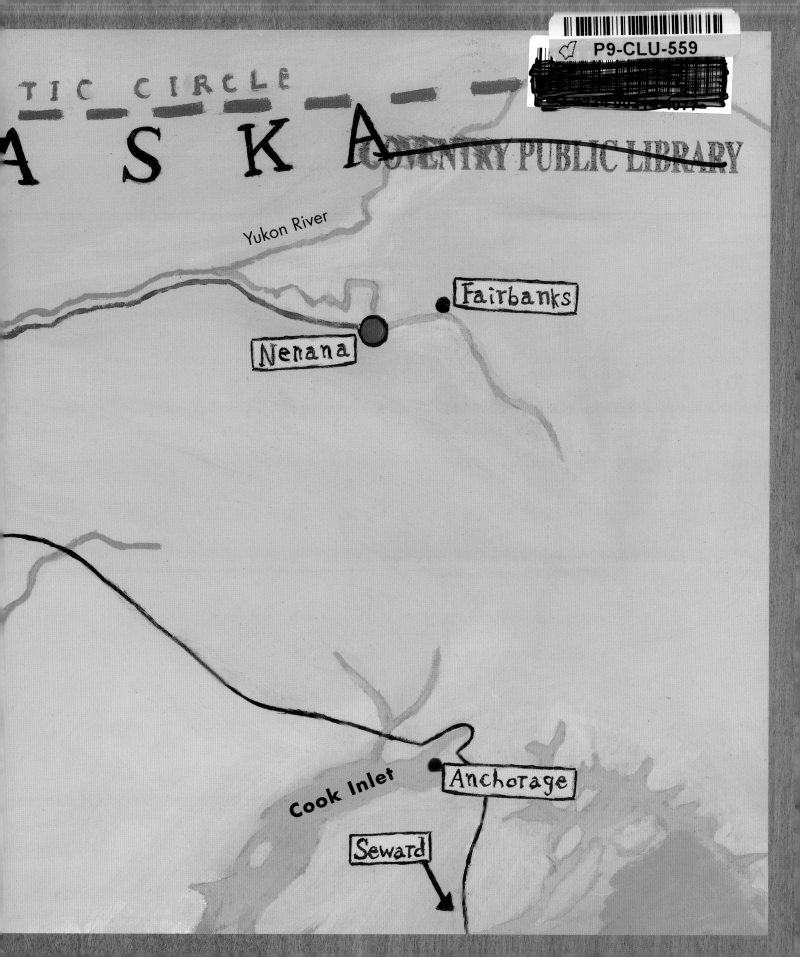

To Dad for bugging me incessantly to do a book about Balto.
After many years, you finally won—so, thanks!

To my uncle Bill for dedicating so much time to this book
by carving the wonderful cover and title page.

To my aunt Sheila and John for letting me use your kitchen table to paint.

To the Blue Rose Girls for your support.
I don't think I could continue to make books without you guys!

To Kaila, my super assistant. I don't know how I'll function without you.

To my aunt Mary for being such a wonderful supporter of my books.
Also, thank you for the entertaining dog stories. I will always think of them and laugh.

Lastly, thank you to my editor, Erin, and designer, Sarah, for not giving up on me,
and to Kate, who stepped in at the last minute. Thank you to everyone
at Random House for doing a wonderful job, as always.

THIS IS A BORZOI BOOK PUBLISHED BY ALFRED A. KNOPF
Copyright © 2011 by Meghan McCarthy
All rights reserved. Published in the United States by Alfred A. Knopf, an imprint of Random
House Children's Books, a division of Random House, Inc., New York.
Knopf, Borzoi Books, and the colophon are registered trademarks of Random House, Inc.
Visit us on the Web! www.randomhouse.com/kids
Educators and librarians, for a variety of teaching tools, visit us at
www.randomhouse.com/teachers
Library of Congress Cataloging-in-Publication Data
McCarthy, Meghan. The incredible life of Balto / Meghan McCarthy.   p.   cm.
ISBN 978-0-375-84460-7 (trade) — ISBN 978-0-375-94460-4 (lib. bdg.)
1. Balto (Dog)—Juvenile literature. 2. Sled dogs—Alaska—Biography—Juvenile literature.
3. Diphtheria—Alaska—Nome—Juvenile literature. I. Title.
SF428.7.M33 2011 636.73—dc22 2009052707
The illustrations in this book were created using acrylic paint on gessoed paper.
MANUFACTURED IN MALAYSIA   August 2011   10 9 8 7 6 5 4 3 2 1   First Edition
Random House Children's Books supports the First Amendment and celebrates the right to read.

THE INCREDIBLE LIFE OF BALTO

MEGHAN McCARTHY

ALFRED A. KNOPF 🐎 NEW YORK

In the remote town of Nome, Alaska, a child was sick. Dr. Curtis Welch was called to his bedside. The doctor had already seen several others sick with a deadly disease called diphtheria and had to hurry if he wanted to make them well again. But he needed medicine that he didn't have—a serum. It was all the way on the other side of Alaska.

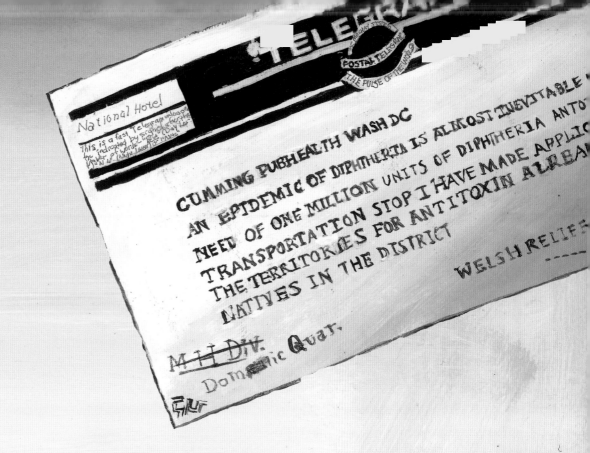

TELEGRAM

POSTAL TELEGRAPH
THE PULSE OF THE WORLD

National Hotel

This is a fast Telegram unless its
deferred character is indicated by a
suitable sign above or preceding the
address.

CUMMING PUBHEALTH WASH DC

AN EPIDEMIC OF DIPHTHERIA IS ALMOST INEVITABLE
NEED OF ONE MILLION UNITS OF DIPHTHERIA ANTO
TRANSPORTATION STOP I HAVE MADE APPLIC
THE TERRITORIES FOR ANTITOXIN ALREA
NATIVES IN THE DISTRICT

WELSH RELIEF

M H DIV.
Domestic Quar.

On January 20, 1925, Dr. Welch sent a telegram:

Nome calling . . . Nome calling . . . We have an outbreak of diphtheria . . .
No serum . . . Urgently need help . . . Nome calling . . . Nome calling . . .

— NOTICE. —

DO NOT ENTER!   This house contains a case of

DIPHTHERIA.

When the danger from contagion has passed this card will be
removed. until further order this house is under hospital regula-
tions, in accordance with Sec. 29. Chap. 14. R.S.

Per Order, **BOARD OF HEALTH.**

...h this card without

A blizzard had swept through Nome, making it nearly impossible to get there. Although two enthusiastic pilots volunteered to attempt the flight, flying in freezing conditions was too dangerous. What would the townsfolk do?

Several days later, a telegram was sent back: *Anchorage calling . . . Anchorage calling . . . 300,000 units of serum located in railway hospital here . . . Could serum be carried to Nome . . . by mail drivers and dog teams?*

Could dogs carry medicine to save the people of Nome?

There was no other choice.

Dogs couldn't make the journey by themselves. People were needed to guide them. Those people were called mushers. The mushers and their dogs would take the medicine in a relay—each team running one part of the journey and then handing the medicine off to the next dogsled team. Twenty teams spread along the route from Nenana (the serum had been sent there from Anchorage) and waited at their posts, ready to race to Nome.

It was fifty below zero when the journey began. Some dogs died on the way because their lungs burst from the cold.

A man named Gunnar Kaasen was chosen as the musher to run one of the last legs of the race . . . and he picked a dog named Balto to be his leader. This was a surprising choice! Balto was inexperienced and not as fast as some of the other dogs. Nobody had ever thought he was special—until now. Kaasen believed in Balto, and Balto proved him right. Balto led the team through blinding snow that pelted their faces. In some places, the snow was so deep that their thin legs hardly moved.

When Balto's team finally got to the checkpoint, the next team was fast asleep. Kaasen figured it would take too long to get them ready for the journey, so Kaasen, Balto, and the team bravely pushed on.

Exhausted and hungry, Balto used his amazing sense of smell to get back on the trail and lead his team onward. Eventually they saw the lights of Nome in the distance. They had made it! Balto delivered the medicine to Nome in record time! "Fine dog," Kaasen said, and then collapsed.

Balto and his team were written about everywhere.
Kids thought Balto was the greatest dog who'd ever
lived. He was a hero!

Balto, Kaasen, and the rest of the team boarded a ship to travel to California, where fans waited to meet the heroic dog. Everybody loved him.

A famous sculptor named Frederick Roth was inspired to make a statue of Balto. Balto stood very still on two chairs inside Roth's studio to pose for the statue. He was very well behaved. When the statue was finished, it was erected in New York City's Central Park. Kaasen and Balto traveled to New York to watch the unveiling.

The statue's plaque read:

Dedicated to the indomitable spirit of the sled dogs that relayed antitoxin six hundred miles over rough ice, across treacherous waters, through Arctic blizzards from Nenana to the relief of stricken Nome in the Winter of 1925.
Endurance · Fidelity · Intelligence

Balto then starred in a silent black-and-white
movie called *Balto's Race to Nome*.

THE HERO DOG AGAIN

"I RAN over...

into the b...
street h...
Vennor ch...
and welc...
month's abs...
say, to a pla...
saw what in...
thing else...
"He was...
followed the...
ner smiled...
asked:
"What was...
you saw in Eng...
the place whe...
aware?"
"Neither," ans...
'thing' at all. I...
You remember...

BALTO HELPS UNVEIL HIS...

Gunnar and 'Balto...
Famous Dog of the
North, at Loew's

While promoting the film, Balto stayed in the world-famous Biltmore Hotel in Los Angeles. At one event, he sat next to the movie star Mary Pickford while the mayor adorned him with a wreath of flowers and gave him a key to the city in the shape of a bone.

Balto, Balto, Balto! He was everywhere!

One company even named dog food after him.

A grapple over money caused the dogsled team to be sold, and Kaasen reluctantly traveled back to Alaska without them. With a new owner, the dogs toured in a vaudeville act. Vaudeville was a kind of entertainment in which a variety of performers such as singers, dancers, and trained animals appeared.

Sadly, Balto and the team were sold again, this time to a man who ran a sideshow. There Balto and the others were all but forgotten. For a dime, people could go into a room and see the once-celebrated dogsled team.

FOOD

A Cleveland businessman named George Kimble paid a dime to see Balto and the other dogs. He remembered the once-famous Balto. How could this have happened? Kimble decided to buy him back. But Balto's owner demanded $2,000, which was a lot of money in 1927. Kimble didn't have enough and was given only two weeks to come up with it!

Kimble wanted to raise the money. With the help of the
Cleveland newspaper, word of Balto's and the other dogs' poor
treatment spread. Children donated their pennies, people passed
around collection hats at their jobs, and stores asked for contributions

Thousands of people gave what they could to help the dogs.
"We just were happy to see that bowl get bigger and bigger,"
said Garnet Bielfelt, whose kindergarten class collected money
to save Balto.

Before long, Kimble had collected enough money. Balto and the others were saved! A headline in the newspaper read: "City Smashes over Top with Balto's Fund!" Cleveland held a parade in Balto's honor, and despite the rain, the citizens were happy.

ALASKA CANADA

WELCOME BALTO!

Kimble donated Balto and his teammates to the Brookside Zoo so that
all of the people who had helped rescue them could visit. Thousands
went to see the dogs on their first day. "I didn't want to see the rest of
the zoo. I just wanted to see Balto," said Garnet Bielfelt. There Balto
could relax and enjoy the rest of his life.

Detective Work

After delivering the serum to the doctor's door that cold winter's night in 1925, Balto became a sensation. Accounts of his heroic deeds were splashed across every major newspaper in the country. The articles, however, contained contradictions and inaccuracies. After doing much research on Balto and the serum run, I was left with two important questions: Was Balto's fur black or brown? And was he even a hero? The book's progress came to a halt. I needed to know what color to paint Balto. I needed to know what really happened. This is when a nonfiction author becomes a detective.

On the subject of Balto's disputed heroism, I read about a man named Leonhard Seppala, a well-known Alaskan musher, who claimed that he was originally supposed to race the entire serum run solo, using his favorite dog, Togo, as lead dog. To Seppala's disappointment, a committee chose twenty mushers to run each leg of the race, deciding that the serum would arrive more quickly that way. Seppala ran roughly five times the total distance of any of the other mushers. Part of the distance Seppala trekked was to receive the serum and the other was during the actual run to Nome. Not running the last leg of the race, however, did not get him, or Togo, the fame he thought they deserved.

This is where the story gets interesting. Gunnar Kaasen did not actually own Balto. Leonhard Seppala did. Balto ran short hauls in the mines and was rarely used for long races. Seppala saw no use for the dog, so he let Kaasen have him for the serum run. And after the great rescue, Seppala didn't think Balto was as deserving of the attention he got as many Americans did, saying, "I was amazed and vastly amused that the dog Balto became a hero."

In 1927, the *New York Times* reported, "Leonhard Seppala, famous musher of the Northwest, declared that a thoroughbred husky named Fox, and not Balto, was leader of his dog team, which rushed diphtheria antitoxin to Nome, Alaska, during the epidemic there in 1925. Seppala stated that Balto had been erroneously proclaimed the hero by the overzealous press agents." Of course this was not true. And the paper also got things so confused that it wrote that Seppala, not Kaasen, was the musher who brought the serum. Seppala later admitted in his biography, "My attention was called to a newspaper report quoting me as saying that Fox and not Balto was the hero of the drive. I hope that I shall never be the man

to take away credit from any dog or driver who participated in that run." Seppala went on to say, in the very next paragraph, that his dog Togo deserved the credit. This is why detective work is very important. Seppala had voiced his opinion so many times that even the *New York Times* got it wrong—and in multiple ways! Some Americans began to form conspiracy theories, writing "wrong dog and wrong serum."

Regarding Balto's statue in Central Park, Seppala said, "I resented the statue to Balto, for if any dog deserved special mention, it was Togo." Perhaps this is why Seppala sold Balto and the other members of his dogsled team after their nine-month vaudeville tour. Togo was obviously Seppala's real love.

Another mystery I needed to solve was what Balto looked like. Some current-day children's books I found depict him as black with white-striped facial markings. Upon examining old photographs of Balto, I discovered that his face, at least in his younger years, was a solid color, with a little white below his muzzle. Also, many modern sources describe Balto as jet-black. I found one firsthand account containing a description of him in a 1925 *Washington Post* article by Albert Payson Terhune. Terhune describes Balto as brown, saying, "I got a good chance to study him. At first glance he isn't flashily beautiful. He is a squat-built dog, only about 22 inches high. He has a rough, dark brown coat and a broad black head with prick ears." It's true that Balto's fur looks black in photographs, but that is because they are not in color. Brown tones can appear black in black-and-white photographs. I was still unsure of what color to paint him. More research had to be done.

After Balto died, he was stuffed and displayed in the Cleveland Museum of Natural History, where he can be seen to this day. If you visit the famous dog, you will notice that he is a mahogany brown. Is this because Balto was a brown dog all along, or did his fur fade over time? I wrote to Harvey Webster, the director of wildlife resources at the museum, to find out. Webster said it was normal for the fur of stuffed animals to fade over time, but he also thought the news article I found was quite compelling. "Since the description from late November 1926 was from an eyewitness, I might be inclined to believe it—that is, that Balto's head was black but the body was very dark brown."

Another piece of information that I needed to consider was the fact that, by most accounts, Balto was a Siberian husky (I found one article in which Seppala, who bred Balto, claimed he was a "cut" dog and not a purebred husky). In my research about the breed, I discovered that Siberian huskies change color frequently, depending on the season and also due to age. I believe it's possible that Balto was not always the jet-black dog that modern sources claim him to be, and for that reason I painted him brown in many illustrations, to match the eyewitness description I had of him.

No matter where information comes from, it gets filtered through many perspectives over time. As a nonfiction writer, I make it my job to take all of the information and piece it together like a giant jigsaw puzzle. But there's more to it than that. I like to choose subject matter that hasn't been covered before or shine a new light on a known topic. Many children's books about Balto tout him as a hero, but none mentions the fact that he was essentially abandoned, sold off, and shown as a live attraction in a dime show. What inspired me about Balto's story was the happy ending after all his struggles. I knew that the whole story needed to be told.

Activities

What do you do when the people you are writing about are no longer alive? Nonfiction authors rely on newspaper articles and books and, most recently, websites to learn about their lives. But how accurate are those sources? Not as accurate as you may think! This is why many authors use the "three" rule—it means that unless your research is really reliable, then usually finding the same information in *three* places is the best rule to go by. For example: If one book says that an alligator was twenty feet long, then you should find that same information in at least two other places.

What if you are going way back in time? What if you are researching an event such as a parade instead of something that can be measured? One person might say the parade was great, but someone else might say it was boring. Some things are simply a matter of opinion! And sometimes opinions and facts get blended together, especially when you are dealing with historical events.

Have you heard of the telephone game? If not, this is how to play it: Sit in a circle with your friends. Whisper a message to the person sitting next to you. Tell that person to whisper the message to the person sitting next to them, and so on. The bigger the circle, the more garbled the message will be at the end. Also, the longer the message is, the more mixed up it is likely to get. Try it! This is the way history can sometimes be.

Here's another activity to try: Form two groups of people. One group will be the "actors" and the other group the "reporters." Actors: Imagine a scene or event of your own invention—be creative! Plan this out in secret. When ready, act out your planned event in front of the reporters. Reporters: Have a pad and pencil ready to describe what the actors are doing. When you're finished, share your reports in front of everyone. What are the differences between the reports? What is the same? No two people see things the exact same way, which explains why there were conflicting news stories about Balto. How would *you* report on the story of Balto? Do you think he was a hero?

Selected Bibliography

Books
Ricker, Elizabeth M., with Leonhard Seppala. *Seppala: Alaskan Dog Driver.* Boston: Little, Brown and Company, 1930.
Salisbury, Gay, and Laney Salisbury. *The Cruelest Miles: The Heroic Story of Dogs and Men in a Race Against an Epidemic.* New York: W. W. Norton & Company, 2005.

Newspaper Articles
"Balto, Dog Hero of Dash to Nome, Is Dying at Zoo," *Cleveland Plain Dealer,* March 10, 1933.
"Balto Helps Unveil His Own Statue," *The Boston Daily Globe,* December 17, 1925.
"Balto, His Husky Pals and Master Get Film Contract," *Cleveland Plain Dealer,* February 26, 1925.
"Balto Not Nome Hero Dog. Seppala Says Husky Named Fox Was Leader of His Team," *The New York Times,* March 9, 1927.
"Balto Plays Host to 15,000 at Zoo," *Cleveland Plain Dealer,* March 21, 1927.
Display Ad 28, *Los Angeles Times,* October 13, 1931.
"Far North Sends Dogs," *The Washington Post,* September 13, 1925.
"$500 Must Be Raised by Night for Balto," *Cleveland Plain Dealer,* March 9, 1927.
"The Hero Dog Again," *The Washington Post,* November 8, 1925.
"Mush at Zero Is Treat for Balto," *Cleveland Plain Dealer,* January 4, 1928.
"Old Sye, Last of Dogs on Famed Balto Team, Dies," *Chicago Daily Tribune,* March 26, 1934.
"Razing of Balto Statue Asked; Dash to Nome Is Called a Hoax," *The New York Times,* September 25, 1931.
"Snow and 60 Below Meat for Huskies, but Rain—" *Cleveland Plain Dealer,* March 20, 1927.
"The Strand," *The Washington Post,* September 14, 1925.

Radio Shows
"Real Sled Dog Balto Different from Spielberg's Film," *All Things Considered,* National Public Radio, December 26, 1995.

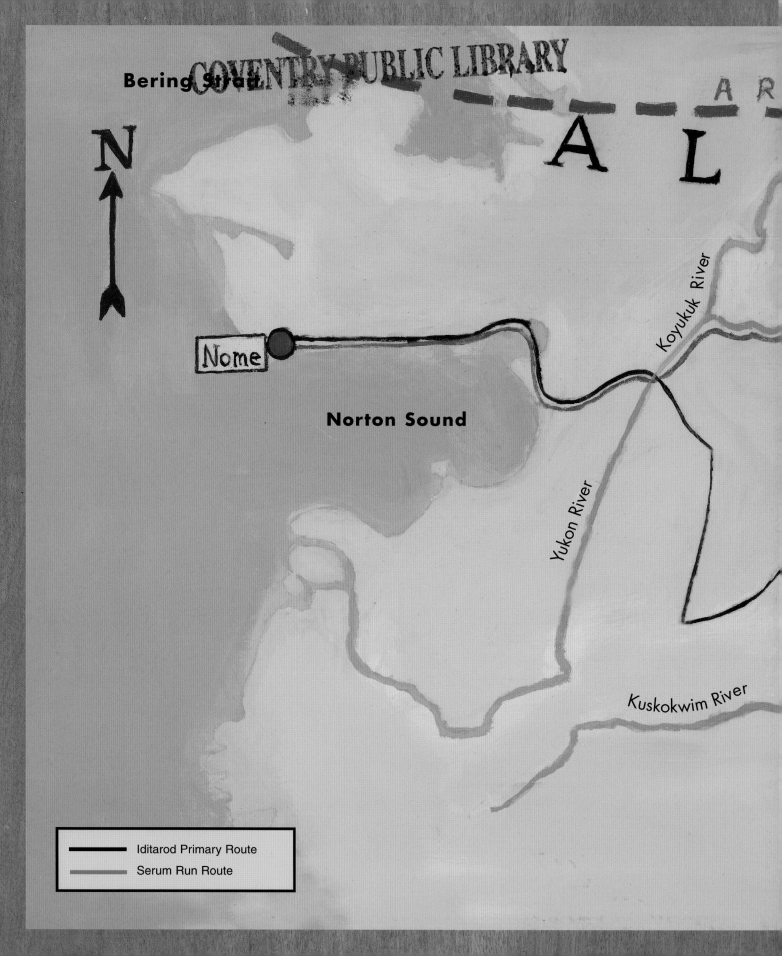

Bering Strait

N

Koyukuk River

Nome

Norton Sound

Yukon River

Kuskokwim River

A
A L
A R

Iditarod Primary Route
Serum Run Route